Your Memory Lingers About Me

love poems

by Karl Stuber

Table of contents

Epoxy of love

The love in my heart, ooh! It's so heavy
    Shore up the supports and strengthen the side
Before love flows out build up the levee
    Find someone's heart, search here, there, far and wide

Need a special heart to do the job right
    Siphon the excess before it's too late
Need a heart that will form a seal that's tight
    Love should always be saved at any cost

In your heart if room is available
    Though currently it's full with love to give
Check and see if our love's compatible
    Remove all the yesterdays with a sieve

Find personalities fit hand in glove
Then we can form an epoxy of love

Empty spaces

I don't want to replace things in your life
　　Just like to fill in the empty spaces
And be a helping hand in times of strife
　　You'll still be around the other faces

All encompassing love is great should it last
　　We shouldn't take a chance on doubts once buried
Caused by moving into our love too fast
　　Emerging sometimes if we get married

You know the way I treat you is kindly
　　When you need, I will handle you with care
But we should not go into love blindly
　　It won't stop the passion from being there

I want love to feel always like the start
I know you are forever in my heart

New ship

My feelings toward you need a bigger ship
   It is a wonderful friendship to trade
For down payment on a relationship
   Just recently it has begun to fade

It's time for something new to take it's place
   Things can't always continue the same way
That is a fact that I can learn to face
   It likely will lead to a brighter day

My heart for collateral to be raised
   Can you see it is in good condition
Where do you go to get a heart appraised?
   Your heart can make the value decision

If time and distance does pull us apart
You'll be able to reprocess your heart

Part of my life

Since twelve I've tried to become "perfect man"
    To use girls for practice I never thought
Learned from complaints by a nearby woman
    Love changes women, men must grow, they taught

Help her in life, don't try to control her
    Picture perfect girls, real women are not
High school dances taught, closely hold partner
    Otherwise shy, girlfriend I never got

Hoped a girl would find me captivating
    Someone who knew the real me through my day
Not learning to date may be a good thing
    Cause it allowed me to meet you, I'd say

Or long ago I would have had a wife
And would miss having you part of my life

Smile so big

I saw a smile so big showed from the back
I thought I did, you saw a passing pup
Looks like a dog whose company you lack
I think, perhaps a pet you couldn't bring up

You're fond of your horse like you love a pet
You lead your horse without holding a line
Invite it along with a smile coquette
Horse hangs head "guys think I'm whupped, okay fine"

Didn't need to care for you to be impressed
It shows you have love and patience galore
Proud to know you, felt a swell in my chest
Never feel anything ulterior

All of my feelings for you are sincere
Except feeling don't miss having you here

Much to learn

There is something I've felt through out my life
So I can give love I have much to learn
With wrong choices in love my past is rife
Although I've known love is something you earn

I've gotten to know someone and their traits
I over analyze I see the end
Reasons it will fail, still believe love waits
Want to never hear I'll still be your friend

Think I've met one who no end will I see
It looks like we will be compatible
And then to love I'll finally feel free
I know with them I feel comfortable

Been trying to get to know them slowly
See no end yet, want to know them fully

Fear me not

You turned and looked not expecting me there
Your wondering eyes met my doting eyes
Yours went yellow receded in the air
What I saw was fear much more than surprise

Fear I can't figure out what to do next
Impressed you so much left a depression
Each time I'm sweet to you now you seem vexed
I'll find a way to end this causation

Fear me not, I know what you're scared to do
Give love and not get any in return
My kind looks and words don't say I'd be true
Actions will show if your love I can earn

I just don't feel our love will go away
Biding time your love I will not betray

Wise

Just what was it you found to become wise
Eyes of a muse in your head shining through
A talk with an old man or group of guys
Views of mountains under a sky pale blue

Did someone open up your heart to love
You saw the possibilities of life
Pulled from the old fears by a hand above
Did you observe things while you lived in strife

Did you feel you were standing in one place
While the rest of the world went rushing by
Had you managed to live at your own pace
What made you suddenly decide to fly

Could it be you have always been this way
I just never noticed until today

Life without limits

Hanging from the moon by a golden thread
With the silver stars shining all around
Wonderment is flowing into my head
All is peaceful I don't notice a sound

Love flowing in my heart keeping it strong
Feeling I have never been this alive
Optimistically it will last long
All that I've been waiting for did arrive

My heart feels free my mind is in order
I recall good times new thoughts I explore
I can approach a life with no border
My heart provides answers if I need more

Life without limits is what I foresee
Enjoying peace of mind and feeling free

You are my world

You're color in a world of black and white
When heard voices are garbled yours is clear
You're a piece of day in the dark of night
You're calm when all others are filled with fear

You're free and clear while others are bogged down
While all others are breaking you just bend
You just lampoon things that make others frown
You stand out in a crowd while others blend

You plan things others live in abandon
Some put others down you pick them back up
You play fair others are running a con
You're the top dog others are just a pup

You're peace and quiet in midst of a storm
When my world is shapeless you are the form

At her request

Subject-matter: buy farm with cow get milk
Patter of feet won't scare me they'd be ours
Satyr: I would not be part of their ilk
Platter of sweets compared to love are sours

Batter-up, I've two outs don't want a third
Chatter says my third girl will be the charm
Matters not didn't get close with, be assured,
Latter girl or first girl, would buy the farm

At her request with first serious one
Bescatter I won't unless she says go
Scatter I would she's found a paragon
Flatter her not her own mind she would know

Attar wouldn't be as sweet to me as would
Smattering kiss from girl in angelhood

Rainbow's end

Although I would say you make the sunshine
Even on a rainy day through the clouds
I've never seen you with a rainbow fine
Folks gather, may have missed you in the crowds

Or are you a leprechaun in disguise
Charged with guarding the gold pot from seekers
At rainbow's terminus they'd need standbys
With your magic filling up your sneakers

Or universe may usurp your beauty
For rainbows and sunsets you've some to spare
Every time around me you're a cutie
With smarts galore and socially aware

From all that I can see and comprehend
I think you are my gold at rainbow's end

First sight

When I found I was attracted to you
It really did come as quite a surprise
You were among some people who were new
Know at dinner we met each other's eyes

Immediately we both looked away
Did see you were someone who could enthrall
Thought I could love a girl like you someday
Then thought it's infatuation that's all

Ignored you after that though you were fine
Didn't think you'd be a romantic prospect
Saw you as a girl in a glossy zine
Then looked at you a way I didn't expect

Talked bout' your name and why I looked so young
Our talk would have made proud Carl Gustav Jung

You're a thinker

Near as I can tell you're sure a thinker
Not just thinker more of a free-thinker
Hope I don't drive you to be a drinker
To other ladies won't be a winker

Help me be a floater not a sinker
At times forget and leave on my blinker
On my van which sometimes is a clinker
I have no tattoos I'm not an inker

When in the pink you make me feel pinker
Glad you never feel I'm a hood-winker
Something's simple broke I'll be a tinker
I'm sure sometimes I can be a stinker

I hope that me being a deep thinker
Does not turn you into a rethinker

I seem the same

The changes you brought about me don't show
I am the only one who can see them
Those who had known me before do not know
I feel they're caught up in ad hominem

And those who have known me as long as you
All think that I have always been the same
When I show my old ways you may construe
That likely I am only being lame

Had been lame was my name, slowed down by fear
Hid it in hard work and learning to bake
Developed character had no one near
Was set in my ways lived for future's sake

I sure don't know how your caring changed me
Set ways turned to dependability

∾

Saving for you

I have no love to give to another
I'm saving it for you for future days
Not counting that which is for my mother
I am sure you have seen it in my gaze

No one else has shown that they notice it
That's a good thing, longing gazes should be
A private thing that is kept in secret
Some day my longing the whole world can see

Those who have seen my poetry do know
There is a lady I deeply care for
Good thing feelings are sincere when aglow
No other will get close, they know the score

I think if ever we become a pair
Poem's sticky sweetness will fill the air

Living quarters

I'd like to buy you a house so fancy
With a plush carpet so deep that you'd sink
Up to your earlobes, hard to be dancy
With legs wrapped in nap, earrings on the brink

Of the surface with hair trailing behind
With a bejeweled tiara on your head
Pushing a huge vacuum a master mind
Had built for such a occasion, instead

You would be happy on a plain wood floor
With socks on your feet sliding on fresh wax
Right across the room go right out the door
We'd laugh so hard like we were maniacs

But would you enjoy camping in a tent
On a sand beach far away from cement

All I need

Was asked what I look for in a partner
She'd rather have an assist than a goal
Although she'd put others ahead of her
Her needs ahead of mine would make me whole

All I'd need, is to know I bring her joy
And give her all the pleasure that she needs
That's something to make me one happy boy
We'd each be proud when the other succeeds

I would always be glad that she chose me
To be the one that she would come home to
No matter the size it would be cozy
Whether mansion or tent love would be true

We'll fit so well they'll be a mystery
Had our souls met before in history

Invisible rope

Guess long distance relationships are tough
Because of the promises to be kept
Lonely ones feel memories aren't enough
Unless at holding their heart they're adept

People are all the same so you will see
Some of my qualities in another
Like to get to know them you should feel free
Your social life I wouldn't want to smother

Want to be sure picking me was no slip
When we arrive at a day where they'll be
No more distance in our relationship
If feelings survived the distance we'll see

Separation will bring us close I hope
We're bound as if by invisible rope

Rainbow eyes

Wonder if I'd see rainbows in your eyes
If you're misty eyed in sunshine's light show
See your eyes in sunset's purple surprise
Indigo's you, Independent you go

When standing close your eyes reflect my blue
I'll never see them green with jealousy
They're green just the same they were born to you
I wish I had "a rhyme with jealousy"

Hope to not see them yellow anymore
Orange is your color it's happy and bright
Didn't look good in red that would be a bore
I'd outlaw the color that wouldn't be right

You're as beautiful as a rainbow now
Must have known I'd get that in there somehow

Me and my heart

Some tomorrow I won't be around town
If I ever hear you're looking for me
I will be the person tracking you down
So I can find where you would think I'd be

Who do you think I am I wonder now
Someone to stop you from being alone
Or do you listen to me and think "wow"
More likely my voice has become a drone

I think it's getting to the point I fear
Where I do not want to say anything
That I feel cause you may not want to hear
Though we're here to the other we're missing

If you and I can get back to the start
I'd know again you found me and my heart

Know me

You know me better than I know myself
I have told you all I know about me
Like tales in a book taken from a shelf
So to me, a surprise it should not be

That you should be able to notice things
I can't see about me from the inside
Experiences shared by us beings
Understood by yourself is a good guide

My heart was open when I spoke to you
Guess there must have been so much it revealed
You recognized hopes and dreams you had too
Things that wouldn't show if my heart had been sealed

Can tell by your look you feel there is more
To find if you continue to explore

Summer love

Please tread lightly into a summer love
For the sake of your heart and sanity
Days with blue skies nights with the stars above
Kissing there that would be some memory

Is it worth the pain of separation
Could we bear to see promises and plans
Turned into a long distance relation
As the summer goes away with our tans

For now we could just stay friends, I won't mind
In case all others just make you feel bored
Even though they had a chance and you find
You have the feelings we never explored

Come back and see the island you hold dear
Waiting for you, know I'll also be here

Showed me love

I have found a lady who showed me love
The love had been in my heart all along
Waiting to be set free like a caged dove
My love was safe behind bars that were strong

So long since the love had been locked away
I had forgotten the love was still there
So long since someone said come out and play
I had forgotten what it's like to care

Shielded my love so it wouldn't get jaded
The door to my heart was closed but not locked
She turned the handle all the bars just faded
I've a clear path no longer is it blocked

It's like meeting a friend from long ago
That's like someone new you're getting to know

౭〜

Down deep

Some say my poems are what they call deep
As my feelings for you get deeper still
I go below to salvage from the heap
Useful thoughts and feelings memories spill

I find I wish I could purge useless thoughts
Can't be done I'm stuck with all these feelings
Old fears need to be dealt with I've been taught
I'm taking benefit of your healings

Those feelings coming from the deep I'll mine
Sheets of poems for those who understand
And see they're not the only ones who pine
For expressed feelings of heart and heartland

I see a day you'll have all the deep space
Together we'll defeat those fears we'll face

Seal your heart

So many people with a broken heart
Have no time or inclination to love
Resting all the wounds is the place to start
Don't spend too long soon give yourself a shove

Or from your broken heart the love will seep
It's sad your heart will never heal that way
There's no hurry to find a love to keep
You'll get some love by being kind I say

A smile from a passing baby they know
It's just what you need they're glad to provide
Enjoy your life you'll start to feel the glow
Before you know there's someone at your side

Pouring into your heart love you will feel
With a heart full that love will form a seal

Fill er' up

Won't discount the heart-body connection
Wonder if an uplifted heart gets lean
Works better when it's getting affection
Pumping more blood to the muscles with protein

Throw out your chest with pride as you just did
That will get oxygen into your lungs
Deoxyribo Nucleic Acid
It looks like a ladder, build up the rungs

Let's get the hemoglobin nice and strong,
Get heart fit, that's the heart of red blood cells
Spread those all around then it won't be long
Til' soon your muscles grow, weakness that quells

Your smile will fill er' up, my heart will thank
Affection will not over flow my tank

Lonely left

If somehow you find lonely at your side
Have him tell about fun times he would spoil
He'd tag along when I'd go for a ride
Lofty mountains we'd hike, he'd like the toil

We'd see great views and sunsets at the shore
But something was missing and I'd feel blue
He made me feel I would enjoy it more
If only I was with someone like you

And now that I carry you in my heart
I find lonely isn't hanging around me
He's done with me now that we'd made a start
On his plan, making me part of a we

Was better company than those around
Until I looked up and your smile I found

No hurry

Some of my poems have a common thread
People say "who is this woman in here?"
Do you love her she has your heart and head
Don't just yet though to me she does endear

Always heard it takes years to love someone
If it is true love that I do Believe
Must experience rough times not just fun
If it's right together heart's fibers weave

Desire follows respect if it's love
Love built just on desire will fizzle
I've respect for the one I'm thinking of
If together we'll certainly sizzle

I see a good reason not to hurry
Wouldn't want to lose her love in a flurry

Love at first sight

I think love at first sight's a connection
That shows this person may fit your ideal
You recognize your own soul's reflection
Looking at them you know how love should feel

You'll learn you love their personality
Because it fits in so well with your own
Can't be explained with rationality
Being with them you do not feel alone

You know that loneliness you couldn't escape
It did not matter who you were around
Just couldn't find one who's heart was the right shape
To fit yours riding life's merry-go-round

When you find they feel the same about you
That is when love grows up and becomes true

❧

Love is always mysterious

Deciding if to ask you for a date
It may seem like I'm way too serious
I'll let that to be decided by fate
Won't stop love from being mysterious

Do want to be able to not hold back
If a paired couple you feel we can be
Will help to keep romance on the right track
Will seem our knack to love is uncanny

Be one doubt, are we having too much fun
That's not a thing that would cause us to split
I'll always be sure I picked the right one
If life should end up having us commit

But still if you decide it won't work out
I'm able to move on won't hang about

In my heart

It's true when I say I don't miss you "much"
Times when you have to be some other place
Way you smile and speak is with me as such
But I don't do well recalling your face

The you I know I carry in my heart
Cause you know that's where I've created "you"
Don't know if it's the real you it's a start
Surprisingly I recall your gym shoe

In the near future if we should get close
Do not worry if you don't match my dream
I won't wander off or become morose.
If real you's better then my thoughts would seem

I may pass out from the excitation
Please use mouth to mouth resuscitation

Fun Side

I'm not a girl don't know if this is true
Girl can't help her heart, where it leads she goes
Always hoping happiness will ensue
But what happens instead if she finds woe

Smile hurts her to show to one she cares for
She may lose her faith in being loved back
May be tempted to give up on amour
What can she do to get love back on track

She showed his words were important to her
He responded well she saw he liked that
Wouldn't that make him want her for his partner
What else to show her love is where it's at

Maybe she could show more of her fun side
In love that's something that could turn the tide

Not Hot

While gazing at you out on the cement
"There's another one she's hot" said the boy
I sure did object and had to comment
Not with jealousy but it was with joy

"She's not hot she's my friend, I respect her"
I said but then I heard my self backtrack
"Sure she is hot but there is none other
She has qualities other women lack"

A hot woman could cool off in a blink
Who wants a hot woman I want a friend
Later on it gave me something to think
That is hot enough for me in the end

If other women hot is what they got
You're much better I think you're not so hot

Us

I've lost my 's' to you besides my heart
I care more about 'u' then 'us' I feel
I like 'us' the times you smile when we part
You frown, I care about 'u' a great deal

Want a happy 'u' what ever it'll take
If my 's' was doing good wouldn't you smile
I'm proud you won't show me a smile that's fake
You frown or smile I'll love you all the while

Someday we can talk about 'us' and see
If in common you have lost your 's' too
Your frowns may say you're concerned about me
Now wouldn't that be a joke on me and 'u'

Should your 'u' and my 's' get together
All that life dishes out we could weather

Feel respect

Gosh, gee, golly you like me, that's too much
I know it's what I had been trying for
Just wishing maybe you wouldn't mind my touch
I have been afraid of touching before

But you listen so well to things I say
As I'm searching for my honest feelings
To speak to you in a different way
You are one who can break through glass ceilings

I have that much respect for you (you're sweet)
I have hoped to feel this way from the start
Always looked for it in ladies I meet
The respect I feel has taken my heart

I have shown it to you a hundred times
So to be with you in different climes

Feel free

You are so very beautiful and kind
I thought I'd let others enjoy your looks
I just felt like learning about your mind
I'm Hoping it is like mine filled with books

Always had yearnings for ladies like you
I had lately decided to rest it
But just then your smile emerged from the blue
I didn't adjust, did not mean to test it

Because soon I felt our souls touch so much
I felt my mind start to sharpen and shine
Felt a tangible warmth without a touch
Started to feel like our hearts could align

I never want to call you mine to own
I feel no need to call you hon or dear
But I never want to say you have flown
I want when you are gone to feel you're near

You should know I do want you to feel free
I hope you will spend that freedom with me

Let her be happy

Thought bout' things I'd do when I got married
If my wife wanted a dog I'd say no
It would just make our life seem too harried
It might leave less time for our love to grow

But after meeting you don't feel like that
Feelings have become important to me
If I'm with someone I'll say "where's it at"
When she says we'll get a dog almost free

That is something not worth fighting about
Letting her be happy would help love's growth
Making her pout not something I would tout
Let her be happy should be marriage oath

Some might think in love you must keep control
But I'll be happy to let the love flow

❧

Love well

Living well is the best revenge I've heard
But when a love may not have gone your way
Got treated badly by one of the herd
Loving well is the best revenge I say

Finding one whose available is tough
You always take a chance on being spurned
There's worry about being treated rough
Especially if you have just been burned

A reason a love may have failed you know
They may have loved themselves too well
I know you can learn to love yourself though
If on past thoughts you don't let your mind dwell

You can learn to forget the way you feel
Even if you can't forgive you're past love
On rebound it's hard finding love that's real
When there is a dark cloud hanging above

Create separation start love anew
Hang with friends clear your mind shouldn't sit and stew

Half life

Always been girl crazy now I'm girl sane
All my life I have felt like half a man
Who's been operating with half a brain
That has all changed since you've become my fan

Functional is how I feel around you
Dysfunctional a love affair might be
That could change in time I'll give you your due
Cognizance and cogitation like me

It took me fifty years to get to that
Twenty five is how old you look, I've seen
Emotions of a thirteen year old brat
Like a six year old to learn you are keen

You have confidence of a three year old
To end, like a baby, your smile is gold

Women like confidence

Be near some women you will hear their sighs
Many have something to complain about
Their boyfriends were hanging out with the guys
When the woman thought he should take her out

About their old beaus they have a complaint
The women said all those guys were boring
They know they were treated as by a saint
The looks the guys gave them were adoring

How they acted to her when they dated
Like she was a princess in a fable
It seems loyalty is underrated
Nice guys bore her being dependable

Some women like guys who are arrogant
Because it shows the guy is confident

Thoughts of you

It's true that I think about you a lot
More than anyone I have ever met
Often things I should have done but forgot
Your eyes and smile that I do not forget

Made an attempt not to think about you
Um, you see, that didn't work out very well
I felt a great loss didn't know what to do
The worst second of my life I do tell

Thinking about you is a pleasant thing
Seems in my head thoughts of you are hard wired
Circling around my brain in a ring
Your thoughts give me strength they don't make me tired

Thinking of you World's a beautiful place
And my future is a good thing to face

෧෧

Love's deferment

We didn't lose at love as it may appear
We can call it more of a deferment
Our number will come around that is clear
Souls fit together yet no commitment

Life may be full of troubles in past days
But future days are clear like a blank page
For us to fill in with our love ablaze
We'll go forward together with courage

Each other's ways we'll have the time to learn
With patience we'll each watch the other grow
We've seen friends fall in love we'll have our turn
We'll get a better fit taking it slow

I'll take time to explore feelings with you
Our love won't age it will remain brand new

Island is weeping

The island is weeping, does it miss you?
Water flowing down being trapped by roads
Finds a low spot, flow continues anew
It needs to be told don't cry, let's send toads

The message needs to get out, cry no more
We will tell it you wouldn't want it that way
Must live life though the island you adore
We'll let it know they'll be another day

You can learn and grow, It thinks you're complete
It wouldn't mind you staying on, not at all
Not as understanding as folks you meet
When your heart listens you might hear it's call

I won't cry I know you exist and how
You've shown I exist too, I'm good for now

〜

Terms

I say I live my life on my own terms
What exactly is meant by saying that
If I don't like my job there's other firms
I don't like my bald head I'll wear a hat

Said you can't have your cake and eat it too
I think you can if you just take small bites
Settle for a lot less is what you do
Live self-deprived lifestyle give up small fights

Call it a equitable solution
Love's compromises helped bring me to you
We'll get what we need in our relation
We are alike differences are few

Wouldn't mind living by your terms for a while
Think I'd like that I'll defer to your style

❧

I save flowers

Some desecrate flowers to guess true love
I need not hurt any flora to play
Nor do I need any help from above
She loves me then she loves me not I say

Alternatively each time I see you
First I have a feeling that can't be beat
Next, the look you give me makes me feel blue
Those times can't wait til' the next time we meet

In consequence eye to eye we don't see
Could it be I could be the cause of that
Self-fulfilling prophecy it may be
Truth is when I'm glad I hide like a rat

To protect the wonderful way I feel
Hope we end on a she loves me for real

Lovefalls

Looking in your eyes I see a pure white
True as the kindness and caring you show
Green, between winter's pine a green so bright
And green of a lake, a color you know

Pupils like rock tunnels to adventure
I imagine travel through a canyon
Beautiful weather carved rock walls ensure
Intricate curves and hues show in the sun

It widens and turns into a meadow
With canyon walls retreated a distance
Reveals flowers colors of a rainbow
The wind's music inviting them to dance

Water falls from walls for a lake to catch
Replace water with love your soul would match

Puppets

Unable to perceive controlling hand
Whether we feel we have it together
Or admit flying by seat til' we land
We go through life thinking we've no tether

Are we only just puppets in a show
Some are in a solo show, that is me
Those in a pair have a partner they know
They may have learned what the next scene will be

Show's over when dating girls guess next act
Often one in a pair have lines down pat
While the other one ad-libs with less tact
I ad-lib, would want partner to do that

To join your act I'd like an audition
Our partnership would come to fruition

Hearts contact

What some couples call love is really not
It's mostly the meeting of body parts
Count the times we touched it was not a lot
Unless you count the touching of our hearts

The times we touched you could count on one hand
I recall the times our hearts made contact
Count our fingers and toes and then expand
To hands and feet of our moms and dads, fact

What we had no one could call love just yet
The feelings were more than I could expect
From any one I've known before we met
Truth is mostly for you I feel respect

When around you I never felt inept
For now what life gives me I can accept

Touch

I shirk from human touch
That which I crave so much
Just how can this thing be
Can someone set me free

I need to break this spell
That's from the bowels of hell
Maybe I need a kiss
And from a charming miss

What I want I confess
Something that may seem less
That which I crave so much
Which is your gentle touch

Future sunsets

Sunset is inferior to sunrise
I've said before but not by very much
Sunrise is equal to a good surprise
And nothing beats love and a loving touch

Sunrises are a brand new beginning
Hope is reborn on a bright shiny day
To see emerging sun is breathtaking
Watch a rising sun and enhance love's play

Sunsets are end of day celebration
It tends to set the stage for scenes of love
And it is found all over the nation
Can be rare sometimes days with clouds above

For now I'll live with hope from the sunrise
Of future sunsets with love in my eyes

Feel your smile

I've seen your smile out the back of your head
Is something I've said in a poem past
But here is something I have never said
Felt your smile, back of my head, like a blast

When I ran by you going fast for real
Didn't speak, last time I saw you, you were mad
Me wearing a lampshade mad, no big deal
Still did not disturb you, but if I had

Would have missed feeling your smile thru my skull
Felt my heart lift like times I saw your smile
It feels as if on my heartstrings you pull
Felt it down a street and across an aisle

Feel it cross land you'd drive in a halfday
Might feel it around the world or halfway

෴

Am I dreaming

Can you pinch me to check if I'm dreaming
This seems to be almost too good to be true
The feelings you have for me are showing
I say almost, I've been waiting for you

So it would seem looking at my love life
Accepting nothing except what I want
What I usually end up with is strife
Sometimes girl who liked me felt like an aunt

Her kindness felt more like supervision
Like third grade teacher kept me in boy's zone
I want to feel love not domination
With you times I'm the student don't feel lone

I've lots to learn you're learning too, I deem
Ooh! That left a mark that says you're my dream

Giddiness

Giddiness is an extreme state of fun
That is a real good thing or so I thought
In Medical terms Giddiness might stun
By definition it's a word that's fraught

Someone asks if you're prone to giddiness
Make sure you get definition of that
Might mean fear of heights or have dizziness
Instead of having fun you will get sat

I'm looking for giddiness in a girl
Hope that's all I'd ever drive a girl to
When we're walking she'd give a joyful twirl
Watching her my heart would give a twirl too

Letting go fear is my definition
It's not to let go all inhibition

Strong love

Recently I have recalled from the past
A way that I thought a love could be
It would certainly find if feelings last
Count on meeting again and hearts are free

Meet someone whose heart and yours could entwine
Get close although not close enough to kiss
Take a chance on love dying on the vine
I do realize true love you could miss

I know just because a love could be true
Does not mean it can survive time and space
Nothing to stop being alone and blue
All you have is a picture of a face

Kids don't try this at home unless you scan
Love stronger than a kiss promise or plan

Child man

Child-woman is the right lady for me
I'm a child-man at fifty one
When I was eighteen I was the same, free
Girl for me should be like that, it's more fun

Besides it makes sense in a paired couple
No reason we can't be free together
To each we can be equally supple
Our shared hearts will be our only tether

It is a cliché when one in a pair
Sometimes complains the other didn't grow up
Hope I would not have that complaint to air
I'm more likely to call her buttercup

I think I'm likely to be more childish
In a pair, she'll likely be womanish

Apple of your eye

I'm looking into your soul through your eyes
I don't see anything to dissuade me
I feel the owner of the soul is wise
From the patience that has been shown to me

I look further into your pupils dark
See a dog, is it yours or just a stray
It may have followed you home from a park
It's yours instinctively knows I'm okay

It's the apple of your eye I might think
If it's a guard dog glad I got by it
As I continue on, deeper I sink
And what I see next will be our secret

However much my readers may cajole
I won't divulge what I see in your soul

Emotions on paper

Some wish I could write about different things
More poems about butterflies and trees
Rainbows in the sky and dragonfly wings
I'd rather write about the birds and bees

Tried to write about my love for nature
To me those poems seemed a little flat
I was afraid of cliches to be sure
Can't always pull a phrase out of a hat

The camera puts on ten pounds they say
Emotions lose half when down on paper
Love has emotion to spare least my way
Flow of emotions had yet to taper

Show my whole love for nature would be fair
Whole love emotions knocks you out your chair

❧

Gushy stuff

Is this why men deny their emotions
To prevent gushy stuff from coming out
Or else that would sure cause some commotions
Women wouldn't know what it was all about

"I love you's" coming from the left and right
Men writing about pups and a kitten
How love waits impatiently for the night
And how for their women they are smitten

Just think what a different world it would be
Poetry sections in your hardware store
Change your oil get poetry books for free
Would some women start to find this a bore

Those women would want their men to be tough
They'd let their men know they had quite enough

Postcard to a poet

Made the mistake and said I write poets
I think it's one of those Freudian slips
Just people with poets in them would get
Putting on paper thoughts slipping from lips

Words that a poet would appreciate
Compares to a mother would love that face
It's something the rest of the world might hate
A better poet would say that with grace

Many have a hidden poet in them
With absolutely no need to be free
Never will flower just remain a stem
Those are people I'm writing to with glee

The weather has been very nice down here
Wish you were here, all would greet you with cheer

Gravity

Although gravity holds us to the ground
We are still living our lives in free fall
No plan, just dealing with what comes around
Using instincts to make a judgment call

Falling from a tall height so far so good
Hoping someone will grab you as you go by
Pick well else they'll let you go as they stood
You'll wonder why some are afraid to try

Everyone falling in all directions
Please say Hi when you fall by me again
If you never see me blame distractions
We'd have to accept it and not complain

Please trust you'll land on your feet like a cat
You sure don't want to fall flat with a splat

Love's wings

Does love have wings? Yes the slim feathers sing
Gently curving up, narrowing at tip
Feathers soft and shining white, joy they'll bring
Muscles with tender sinew I wouldn't clip

Gladly my heart leaps when my love flies free
She gleefully rides the drafts, up she soars
So high her lovely form I cannot see
She lands, wings enfold with love, my heart roars

We embrace, her wings flap, my passion lifts
Soaring above the earth our passion grows
Enjoying the great pleasure of her gifts
Feeling the air as around us it flows

World goes on outside our moment in time
We'll fully enjoy our love at it's prime

Your caring

Yes! Still there, good feelings you left behind
Always like to check after a hard day
All the emotional bonds off my mind
I'm able to think straight, my thoughts don't stray

I have reduced my fears of what may be
New experiences aren't things to dread
Recalling my hopes and dreams I feel free
To fulfill them, thinking with a clear head

Your caring hasn't made me believe in me
That's really something I always have done
Seemed no one I met could see what I see
That made the struggle to succeed no fun

Hard to face the day when folks say you're wrong
That matters no more since you've come along

Need smiles

Felt the need for a smile and looked around
You were passing by and had one to spare
The look on your face said "look what I found".
Had it when I saw you last, left it there

Appreciate you keeping it for me
Was afraid I lost it along the way
A smile is hard to get, though it is free
Could manufacture one with time to play

I'm sure you can give me one of your own
I'll keep it with me so you'll see it's fine
When I give it back you'll see it has grown
Your heart stamp will show it is genuine

In my heart it will be kept warm and snug
With all the feelings of a lasting hug

Get ready

Am I ready, ready to take that step
It's next but I don't feel ready not yet
Lots of get up and go, plenty of pep
My heart's not in it, my mind is not set

What do I wait for? Doubts to go away
That shouldn't be hard because the doubts are mine
Til' they leave I'll fret and worry each day
If I can see where they're from I'll be fine

Don't see the present I just see the past
Times I failed, those memories in my brain
It just tells me it knows that things won't last
But if that is true, doubts can also wane

Man in the mirror looks ready to me
I better get ready, for I am he

Loyalty is underrated

Being reliable is powerful
There for someone, people aren't used to that
Can't really trust someone would be thoughtful
Just hippies say kindness is where it's at

It seems loyalty is underrated
Being kind is seen as a shortcoming
Today's world thoughtfulness has abated
Being dedicated isn't becoming

Trying hard to please you're excitable
Get a grip on yourself, better calm down
Trying to help you'll be expendable
Pouring on kindness you'll make someone drown

But helpful people are a lifesaver
You need your life saved I'll do that favor

Inner strength

If you have inner strength you can be kind
Those who are weak, surliness they will show
If you are strong something that you wouldn't mind,
Leaving yourself vulnerable, you know

You would just not be afraid to allow
People pass your defenses that exist
You can deal with it later you know how
One in trouble you'll be glad to assist

On a limb, most people just won't go out
You won't think twice about lending a hand
It's the least you could do cause you're about
For the downtrodden you will take a stand

When watching this I see you at your best
Cause to improve the world is a good quest

Spinning tops

In life if not puppets, we're spinning tops
Recall when you've spun tops on a table
Touch affects tops direction, some do flops
In life, contact with folks makes us able

With no catalyst we'd just spin in place
We would never improve, wouldn't join the game
The accomplishments that we all embrace,
If we can attain a measure of fame

That is due to others touching our life
With sense of belonging and wherewithal
With solitude a hermit escapes strife
But nothing he does brings progress at all

You can change the situation you're in
Strong and flexible can control your spin

∽

You've got dibs

Is it you I've been waiting for these years
Never felt this comfortable before
Does not mean I still won't be faced with fears
Can accept your friendship and not want more

That would be unnatural and unfair
To you if not to me, that stunts progress
You might meet one who will show they care
And the friendship you show me will be less

Without your heartfelt smile I wouldn't be fine
Saved for a special one less for a friend
That would encourage me to make you "mine"
I'd love to be your special one we'll blend

My intention, to hold my heart for you
Glad to wait to find if this love is true

Heads spin

I encourage passion with the right one
Passion is something I've wanted to find
But for the sake of love not only fun
Does love start with two people being kind

Gently gazing eyes build a smile you know
Mix in giggles and belly laughs to taste
Take that and tend it with care, watch it grow
We will both be sure to prune out the haste

Eyes wide, we wouldn't want our love to blind us
Or we may lose sight of the world we're in
And get hit by a metaphoric bus
If not a real one, heads in the clouds spin

Long as new love's feelings we're reliving
To each other our love we'll be giving

Hollow heart

When a woman meets a man she could love
She will then clear her heart out to make room
Hoping his heart will fit her's like a glove
He'd jump right in is something she'd assume

But what if he is a little bit slow
To show the love for her she knows is there
Wouldn't he want to go out and see her glow
Doesn't everyman need a woman to care

These doubts appear, she feels a hollow heart
Too soon her love wears a facade of hate
When he notices he will try to start
He will soon realize it's way too late

Usually here I would make a bad pun
Ladies hearts mean too much, I can't make fun

Tear duct therapy

Your eyes water from some of my poems
Then I have accomplished my objective
Tear duct therapy, I could write proems
For books on dry eyes, it's no way to live

Had looked for things to bring tears to my eyes
Fix my ducts, happy sentimental tears
Tears at weddings, not tears when someone dies
Romantic comedies — Do I hear jeers?

It's that guy reading over your shoulder
I know he'd cry if some gears he heard grind
Tears are in the eyes of the beholder
Sports themed romantic comedies, eyes blind

Slightly with tears, I guess when I'm a groom
They'll mop up the tears, won't do with a broom

No losers without winners

I see winning is so overrated
It's not making the world a better place
This is a concept that is outdated
I'd rather see a smile on every face

I've competed in races for four decades
Upper echelon but the lower ranks
There the camaraderie never fades
Was self-improvement at each other's flanks

To me a win is being satisfied
With my strategy and preparation
I've won, was scary being glorified
How can you not change with adulation

To me winning is when peace wins a war
I do not think the world needs any more

Left over phrases

These free to a good home, phrases that failed
I often jot down what seems a good thought
Try to make a poem, on these I've bailed
Yours if you want, might be a phrase you sought

"Lost motivation, momentum's all's left"
Not a happy thought, can't find it work here
"You're in my heart , feel we're winning" not deft
Ripped on winning, that line would seem a jeer

"Future actions, body-language misleads"
Bod's language, Psycho-babble anyway
"Beautiful woman can't find love she needs
The fear of losing her is in man's way"

"Have no faith, it's tied in a long term bond
No faith for another, for one I'm fond"

Shown respect

One thing that folks do that makes me lonely
Is to decline to give their opinion
I had asked to show my respect only
I suspect it is to show dominion

But they'll give their opinion when not asked
Sounds like I have a pet peeve, not really
People should let their respect be unmasked
Respect you have for me is shown freely

Nothing you do makes me feel peeved at all
Your opinions are appreciated
Towards me you're not dictatorial
To show you respect I'm dedicated

When I get your opinion I figger'
I am really part of something bigger

Saw your soul, missed you

I just do not always recognize you
Those times when you pass by me in the street
The friendship that we have still seems like new
We have good conversations when we meet

The look in your eyes is what I recall
Also the smile on your face when we'd talk
Your face I do not remember at all
I do not know how you look when you walk

What I notice are the thoughts on your mind
And the way you listen to what I say
The comments that you make are always kind
Seeing you tends to brighten up my day

I forgot how you look on the outside
But I feel I know you on the inside

Made in the USA
Charleston, SC
22 May 2011